Veggie Mania®

by

Cathy Prange

and

Joan Pauli

Third Printing

November 1986

Published and Distributed by
Muffin Mania Publishing Co.,
553 Greenbrook Dr..
Kitchener, Ontario. N2M 4K5

Printed by Ainsworth Press
Kitchener, Ontario

Veggie Mania

You loved our muffins,
You loved our nibbles,
You'll love our veggies too!
Our book is filled
With garden greens,
And they are good for you!

Can you believe this? Now we
are writing poetry! That doesn't
mean we're tired of making muffins and
nibbles, it's still great fun! This
just seemed to be a good way to introduce
our new book, "Veggie Mania".

Many of you have been asking,
"What's next"? Well, here it is!
Your tremendous support over the last
four years has forced us out of the
Office and back into the Kitchen (only
kidding, we never really left!) Instead
of spending all Friday morning in the
kitchen, we are now in the supermarkets
hovering around the produce counters,
filling our carts with veggies.

Our Research Department (us) has
worked very hard to determine the
biggest meal-time dilemma, and the
resounding response was "veggies"!
Therefore, in keeping with today's
lifestyle, we have tried to give you
delicious, easy to prepare, recipes.
With two Canadian Best Sellers and
La Manie des Muffins aussi, it is more
important than ever to be organized!

Have a Meal Plan like a Game Plan! Why be stuck in the kitchen missing the fun (and cocktails)? After all, guests do not feel comfortable entertaining themselves.

You'll love our Veggie Mania! There is a vegetable for everyone's taste and for every occasion.

We had fun doing it! You'll have fun using it!

Sisters, Partners, and

Still Best Friends,

Cathy Monge

Joan Pauli

Hints

Eat, drink and be merry
Is a symptom of our day,
Be sure of healthy eating
The Veggie Mania way!

1. Most of our top-of-the-stove veggies may be made ahead, placed in a greased casserole and reheated in your oven or microwave.

2. It is easier and more economical to substitute powdered chicken or beef broth for canned broth.

3. To Gild a Lily – pour a little melted butter and grated lemon rind over cooked, fresh veggies.

4. Mix left-over mashed potatoes with an egg and 1 tbsp. flour, roll in cereal crumbs and chill on a greased cookie sheet until ready to bake. Tastes better than a mashed potato sandwich!

5. Remember our Lunch or Brunch muffins will compliment your soups and salads!

6. If you have peeled more potatoes than you want to cook – cover them with some water with a few drops of vinegar added. They will keep 3 or 4 days in your refrigerator.

7. Never discard parsley or celery leaves – remove all branches and dehydrate in microwave for 4 min. turning once. Crumble and store in covered jar.

Table Of Contents

Table Of Contents continued:

Table of Contents continued:

Table Of Contents continued:

Soups

Soups, salads & make-aheads
Are oh so easy to do,
And the best part of our
Veggie Book
Is that they are _good_ for you!

Doris' Borscht

2 1/2 lbs. Spare Ribs

3	cups beets (cut into strips)
2	cups beet leaves and stems (cut up)
2	cups shredded red or green cabbage
1	sliced carrot
1	stick of celery, or 3/4 cup with a few leaves
1	large onion, chopped
1	cup canned tomatoes (or 1 cup of fresh)
1	clove garlic, crushed
1	tsp. chopped parsley
1	tsp. chopped dill weed
3	tsp. salt
1/2	tsp. pepper
2 1/2	tsp. vinegar
2	tbsp. flour
2	tbsp. butter
1	cup sour cream

Method

Boil ribs for 3 minutes. Drain and rinse in cold water.

Now we start the borscht.
Bring 12 cups of water to a boil, drop in the ribs, and boil for 5 min. Add all the ingredients except the butter, flour and sour cream.

Boil until the spare ribs are nearly tender, then lower heat.

continued on next page .....

1

Doris' Borscht (continued)

Melt the butter on low heat in a
frying pan and roast flour with the
butter until light brown. Add 2
cups of soup to this mixture and
boil a few minutes. Add to the pot
of soup while it is boiling on low
heat and boil about 3 minutes
longer. Let the soup cool.

Take 2 cups of soup and put it into
another pot. Cool completely. Add
the sour cream to this, blending it
together. A tablespoon of milk will
help to blend it.

Add this to the cooled soup. The
soup should not be boiled after the
sour cream mixture has been added.

Heat and serve.

This soup tastes much better after it
has been sitting aside for 6 hours.
It even tastes better the next day.

Note: You will notice throughout the
method, cooled soup is mentioned
several times — cooling the soup
prevents curdling.

This borscht tastes best when using
fresh beets and also freezes well.

You won't believe what a delicious
"one-pot meal" this hot soup is!

To serve, remove ribs and serve
on the side!

2

Cabbage Soup

1	lb. ground beef
1	medium onion, chopped
1/2	c. diced celery
1/2	green pepper, chopped
2	tbsp oil
2	tsp salt
2	tbsp sugar
1/4	tsp pepper
	dash paprika
1	28 oz can tomatoes
2	5 1/2 oz cans tomato paste
4	c. hot water
2	beef bouillion cubes
3	tbsp parsley flakes
1	large potato, diced
2	carrots, diced
1	small head cabbage, coarsley chopped.

In large soup pot, sauté ground beef, onion, celery and green pepper in oil until beef is browned (breaking up while browning).

Add remaining ingredients except cabbage and combine thoroughly. Simmer uncovered for 1 hour, stirring occasionally.

Add cabbage. Combine and simmer covered for one hour.

If too thick, add more hot water.

A good, nutritious meal in a bowl!

3

Louise's Cream of Carrot Soup

```
1/3 cup butter
1/2 cup chopped onions
2    cups sliced carrots (3 med.)
3    chicken bouillon cubes
3    cups boiling water
1/4 cup rice
1/2 tsp. salt
2    cups milk
```

Sauté onions in butter until transparent.

Add carrots and stir until well coated.

Add bouillon cubes, water, rice and salt. Cook until rice and carrots are tender – 20 min.

Place in blender and purée.

(at this point, soup can be made ahead and refrigerated)

When ready to serve, return to pot, add milk and heat.

Cream of Cauliflower Soup

1	large onion
2	tbsp butter or margarine
3	cans chicken broth
2	medium carrots, sliced
1	medium cauliflower, cut into pieces
1	cup cream
	salt and pepper to taste
1/8	tsp nutmeg
1	tbsp sherry
	parsley for garnish

Slice onion and sauté in butter or margarine in large saucepan until limp, about 5 minutes.

Add chicken broth and bring to a boil. Add carrots and cauliflower to boiling broth and simmer covered until veggies are tender - about 15 minutes.

Pureé in blender or food processor.

Return to soup pot and add cream, salt, pepper, nutmeg and sherry. Heat, but do not boil.

Garnish with parsley, croutons, or tiny cauliflowerets.

Serves 6 - 8

Just as delicious when broccoli or asparagus are substituted for cauliflower!

5

Donna's Corn Chowder

1	cup chopped onion
2	tbsp. butter
2	cooked potatoes, diced
2	cups ground or chopped ham
1	19 oz. can creamed corn
1	can mushroom soup
2 1/2	cups milk
3/4	tsp. salt

Sauté onion in butter in saucepan.

Add rest of ingredients and heat just to boiling.

(1 can of flaked ham may be used)

Use your left-over ham in this easy chowder. Men love this one!

For making corn-on-the-cob that stays hot and fresh - use only cold water and, for every 4 ears, 2 tablespoons each of sugar and vinegar. Bring water to a boil, then add corn. Cook for 6 minutes then remove the corn as desired. The corn left simmering in the hot water will stay fresh for hours!

Fresh Mushroom Soup

4   slices bacon cut into small
      pieces
3   tbsps. butter
1   large onion, chopped
2   cloves garlic, minced
2   lbs. mushrooms, sliced
6   tbsps. tomato paste
6   cups chicken broth
4   tbsps. sweet vermouth or sherry
1   tsp. salt
1/2   tsp. ground fresh pepper
      grated mozzarella, swiss or
      parmesan cheese

Cook bacon until brown. Add butter.

Add onion and garlic, and cook until
soft.

Stir in sliced mushrooms and cook
gently for 10 minutes.

Stir in tomato paste.

Add chicken broth, vermouth or sherry,
salt and pepper. Simmer for 10 min.

Pour into soup bowls and sprinkle
with cheese.

Serves 6.

Serve as a change from French Onion
soup!

French Onion Soup

6   medium onions, thinly sliced
6   tbsp butter
1   tsp sugar
1   tsp salt
    dash nutmeg
7   c. beef broth
1/4 c. sherry
6   slices of French bread, toasted,
    or 6 Holland rusks.
    grated swiss cheese
    grated parmesan cheese

Sauté onion in butter until soft.

Add sugar, salt and nutmeg and toss well.

Cook until golden brown. Add broth and bring to a boil.

Simmer 10 minutes and add sherry.

Ladle soup into oven-proof bowls and top with a slice of toasted French bread, or a Holland rusk.

Cover with swiss cheese.

Bake at 300 degrees for 10 minutes.

Add parmesan and broil until cheese bubbles.

Serves 6.

You don't have to be French to like this one!

8

Potato Leek Soup

1 1/2 c. diced leeks (approx. 2)
1/2 c. diced onion
1 clove garlic, minced
4 tbsp butter
4 c. chicken broth
1 1/2 c. diced potatoes
1 c. heavy cream
salt and pepper to taste
chopped green onions

Sauté leeks, onion and garlic in butter until transparent.

Add broth and potatoes and bring to a boil. Cover and simmer until potatoes are tender, about 15 min.

Pureé in blender or food processor.

Return to large saucepan and add cream, salt and pepper.

(If soup is too thick, add more cream or broth)

Garnish with chopped green onions.

Serves 8.

A tasty prelude to your gourmet dinner – delicious hot or cold.

Salads

Three Bean Salad

1 14 oz can green beans
1 14 oz can yellow beans
1 14 oz can kidney beans
1 19 oz can chick peas
1 medium onion, chopped
1 green pepper, cut in small pieces

Marinade:

In a small bowl mix:

3/4 c. white sugar
2/3 c. white vinegar
1/2 c. vegetable oil
1   tsp. salt
1/2 tsp. pepper

Drain the beans and the peas.

In a large bowl mix the drained beans
and peas, chopped onion, green pepper
and the marinade.

Refrigerate one day before use.

Store in covered jars in the
refrigerator.

Drain before serving.

An all time favourite for any
occasion. An easy make-ahead that
compliments any meal.
Take to your next Pot Luck Supper!

Beet Mold

1 14 oz can crushed pineapple
1 14 oz can diced harvard beets
3 tbsp. white vinegar
1 tsp. onion salt
2 small pkgs. wild cherry jello

Drain juice from pineapple and beets.
Add water to juice, if necessary, for
3 cups of liquid.

In medium saucepan heat the juice,
vinegar and onion salt.

Stir in and dissolve the 2 pkgs. of
wild cherry jello.

Chill juice until slightly thickened
and then add pineapple and beets.

Pour into bowl or mold and let set.

We find this colorful mold is delicious
served with any meat.
Try this instead of cranberries with
your roast turkey or chicken!

Janie's Broccoli Salad

1   bunch broccoli, cut into spears
1/2 lb. bacon, cooked, drained and
    crumbled
1   c. shredded cheddar cheese
1   onion, chopped, or 4 green onions,
    chopped.

Place all ingredients in bowl and
toss with dressing.

Dressing:

Mix together,

1   c. salad dressing
1/4 c. white sugar
2   tbsp. vinegar

Serves 6 - 8

If you're bored with cabbage salad,
try this!
Certainly a hit with our family and
guests.

Mother Milner's Horseradish Mold

1   pkg. unflavored gelatin
1/4 c. cold water
1/4 c. hot water
1/2 c. sweet pickle juice
2   tbsp lemon juice
1/2 c. drained horseradish
1/2 c. mayonnaise
1/2 c. chopped celery

Dissolve gelatin in cold water.

Add hot water.

Add pickle juice, lemon juice, and drained horseradish. Allow to partially set.

When partially set, fold in mayonnaise and chopped celery.

Pour into mold or glass dish.

No sneezing at your dinner table with this one!
A super, mild accompaniment for your roast beef!

Layered 24 hr. Veggie Salad

1 head lettuce, torn
1 tsp. white sugar
  salt and pepper to taste
6 hard-cooked eggs, sliced
1 10 oz. pkg. frozen peas, thawed
1 lb. bacon, crisp cooked and
  crumbled
2 cups shredded swiss cheese
1 cup mayonnaise or salad dressing
  sliced green onions with tops,
  (optional)

In bottom of large salad bowl, place
3 cups of torn lettuce.

Sprinkle with sugar, salt & pepper.

Layer sliced eggs on top of lettuce,
standing some eggs around edge of
bowl. Sprinkle with a little salt.

Next, layer in order:

Thawed peas, remaining lettuce,
crumbled bacon and shredded cheese.

Gently spread mayonnaise over the top,
sealing to the edge of the bowl.

Cover and refrigerate 24 hours or
overnight.

Garnish with sliced green onions and
tops, if desired.

Toss just before serving. Serves 12-15

Make Ahead Layered Salad

1   head lettuce
1/2   head cauliflower, broken into
        bite-size pieces
1   lb. bacon, cooked and crumbled
3   medium green onions, chopped
2   c. salad dressing
1/4   c. white sugar
1/3   c. parmesan cheese

Layer lettuce, cauliflower, bacon and
onion in large salad bowl.

Mix salad dressing with sugar and
parmesan cheese. Spread over greens
and seal to edge of bowl.

Refrigerate overnight and toss just
before serving.

Serves 10

Both our make-ahead layered salads
are great for your buffets, or for
salad lovers, a meal by itself served
with our hot luncheon muffins!

Julia's Fresh Mushroom Salad

1 head romaine
1 head of lettuce
1/2 lb. fresh mushrooms

Line a salad bowl with romaine leaves.

Tear rest of romaine and head lettuce into bite-size pieces.

Wash, trim and slice mushrooms, and combine with lettuce.

Toss with dressing and place in romaine-lined bowl.

Dressing:

1/2 cup oil
1/4 cup vinegar
1/4 cup chopped green onion
1/4 cup parsley
1 tbsp. chopped green pepper
1 tsp. white sugar
1 tsp. salt
1 tsp. dry mustard
1/8 tsp. cayenne pepper

Beat all with beater or shake well in tightly covered jar. Store in refrigerator.

Shake well before serving. Serves 4-6

Ladies! A great luncheon salad!

Maureen's Dilly Onion Rings

1   large Spanish onion, thinly
     sliced and separated into rings.

Combine:

1/3 c. white sugar
2   tsp salt
1   tsp dillweed
1/2 c. white vinegar
1/4 c. water

Stir until sugar dissolves.

Pour over onion rings, cover and
refrigerate at least 5 hours.

Stir occasionally.

(May be made 1 or 2 days before
 needed)

Drain and serve.

This takes the "hot" out of onions.
A super side dish for special occasions
or your family barbecue!

Sauerkraut Salad

1 28 oz can sauerkraut, drained
1 19 oz can bean sprouts, drained
2 cups celery, chopped
1 green pepper, chopped
1 pimiento, chopped

Mix all above together.

Sauce:

1 c. vinegar
1 c. white sugar

Boil sauce for 3 minutes, cool and pour over sauerkraut and vegetables.

Refrigerate, covered, until ready to use.

Keeps well.

Another Waterloo County favorite!
Even if you don't like sauerkraut,
you'll love this!

Marinated Veggies (1)

1   can baby carrots, drained
1   green pepper, sliced in rings
1   red onion, sliced in rings
1/2 lb. fresh mushrooms, washed
     and drained well, or
     1 can whole mushrooms, drained
1   cucumber, pared and sliced

Combine veggies and add 1 small
bottle of Italian dressing,
                or
1   pkg. Italian dressing mixed
     with 2 tbsp. sugar, 2 tbsp.
     salad oil and 2 tbsp. tarragon
     vinegar.

Marinate at least 6 hours or
overnight.

Drain and serve.

A vegetable a day keeps the Doctor's
bills away!

Marinated Veggies (2)

1 bunch broccoli, washed and cut into spears.
1 small cauliflower, cleaned and cut into bite-size pieces
1 can whole mushrooms, drained
1 green pepper, sliced
   cherry tomatoes

Place veggies in large bowl and pour one large bottle of Italian dressing over all.

Cover and refrigerate overnight.

Drain and serve.

A colorful side dish for lunch or dinner parties!

Hot Veggie Combos

Simple & Delicious Veggie Topping

1	small onion, grated
1/2	cup butter
1	cup mayonnaise
1	tbsp. horseradish
1	tbsp. prepared mustard
1	tsp. salt
	black pepper or cayenne to taste

Allow butter and onion to soften together (Do not melt).

Add remaining ingredients.

Mix well and refrigerate.

Keeps in refrigerator for a remarkable time.

"Great served over fresh broccoli and asparagus!"

To soften hard butter in a hurry - grate it!

Asparagus Casserole

2   12 oz cans asparagus tips, or
     2 lbs fresh, cooked.
5   hardboiled eggs
1/2 c. grated cheddar cheese
2   c. cream sauce

Layer asparagus, sliced hardboiled
eggs, cream sauce and cheese.

Top with buttered crumbs.

Bake at 350 degrees for 30 minutes
or until hot and bubbly.

Serves 6.

Cream Sauce:

2   tbsp butter or margarine
2   tbsp flour
1/2 tsp salt
     dash pepper
1/2 tsp curry powder
2   c. milk

Melt butter, blend in flour, salt,
pepper and curry powder. Add milk and
cook stirring constantly until mixture
thickens.

Buttered Crumbs:

1   c. dry bread crumbs or cracker
     crumbs.
2   tbsp butter, melted.

No Crust, No Fuss Asparagus Quiche

1	lb. asparagus
2	tbsp. soft butter
1/4	cup fine, dry breadcrumbs
8	slices bacon, or 1 cup diced cooked ham
1	cup grated Fontina or cheddar cheese
3	eggs, beaten
1	cup light cream
1/2	cup milk
	pinch nutmeg
	freshly ground pepper

Cut asparagus into 2" lengths. Cook in boiling salted water until tender-crisp. Drain well.

Spread bottom and sides of a 10 inch quiche dish with the butter.

Sprinkle the breadcrumbs on top and make sure bottom and sides of dish are coated.

Cook bacon until crisp, drain and crumble. Sprinkle over the crumbs.

Sprinkle 3/4 cup of cheese over bacon.

Arrange asparagus over cheese, reserving 6 of the tips for the top.

Beat eggs, cream, milk and seasonings and pour over all. Top with rest of the cheese.

Decorate top with reserved asparagus tips. Bake at 350 degrees for 40-45 min.

Bar-Room Casserole

(Barley - Mushroom Casserole)

1/4 c. butter or margarine
1/2 lb. mushrooms, thinly sliced
1   onion, coarsley chopped
1   c. pearl barley
1/2 tsp salt
1/8 tsp pepper
4   c. chicken broth

Melt butter or margarine and sauté mushrooms and onion for 5 minutes or until tender.

Add barley and brown slightly, stirring frequently. Stir in salt and pepper and turn into a 2 qt. casserole.

Add chicken broth and mix well.

Cover and bake at 350 degrees for 1 1/2 hours. Add more broth, if needed.

Serves 6.

A good substitute for rice with chicken or pork.

You may substitute beef broth for chicken broth if desired, and serve with beef.

And you thought barley was just for soup?

24

Green Bean Casserole

2   pkgs. frozen French-style
     green beans.
1   can water chestnuts, drained
     and sliced
1   19 oz. can bean sprouts, drained
     well.
3-4 green onions, chopped
1   can cream of mushroom soup
1   cup grated sharp cheese
1   can French-fried onion rings, or
     chow mein noodles, or 1 cup of
     chopped almonds.

Cook green beans for half of the
cooking time and drain well.

In a large greased casserole, layer
green beans, water chestnuts, bean
sprouts, mushroom soup and the grated
cheese.

Bake for 30 minutes at 350 degrees.

Sprinkle French-fried onion rings on
top and bake 5 minutes longer.

This casserole may be made ahead of
time and refrigerated.

Serves 8.

Green Beans and Mushrooms

1   lb. frozen french-cut green
        beans.
1   can sliced mushrooms, drained
1   can mushroom soup
1/2 c. milk or cream
        salt and pepper to taste
1   c. breadcrumbs
2   tbsp butter
1/2 c. parmesan cheese

Cook frozen beans according to
package instructions, just until
tender-crisp.

Grease a 1 1/2 quart casserole.

Mix beans with mushrooms, and
mushroom soup which has been thinned
with the cream or milk, salt and
pepper.

Place all in casserole and top with
crumbs.

Bake at 350 degrees for 45 minutes,
or until heated through.

Serves 6.

Crumb Topping:

Melt 2 tbsp butter in frying pan.
Add 1 cup breadcrumbs and 1/2 cup
of parmesan cheese.

Green Beans Oriental

2   14 oz cans cut green beans,
    well drained, or
    2 lbs. frozen green beans,
    cooked as directed and well
    drained
3   stalks celery cut diagonally
    into 1/2 inch slices
2   tbsp butter or margarine
1   tbsp cornstarch
3/4 c. chicken broth
2   tbsp soy sauce
    dash garlic salt
2   tsp toasted sesame seeds

Cook celery in butter or margarine
until tender-crisp.

Blend cornstarch with chicken broth,
soy sauce, sesame seeds and garlic
salt.

Cook with the celery, stirring
constantly until thickened.

Add drained beans and heat thoroughly.

(Could be made ahead and placed in
greased casserole dish and heated
for 30 minutes at 350 degrees)

Serves 6 - 8

Good with chicken and turkey.

Oktoberfest Beans

8	slices of bacon
1	c. finely diced celery
1	c. finely diced onion
1	small can tomato paste
1/2	c. brown sugar
1	envelope spaghetti sauce mix
2	tbsp prepared mustard
1	tsp garlic salt
2	tbsp vinegar
2	cans lima beans, drained
1	can kidney beans, drained
1	28 oz can pork and beans

Cook bacon until crisp, drain and crumble.

Add celery and onion to 2 tbsp bacon fat and sauté for 5 minutes.

Add 1 cup of water and all other ingredients, except beans. Bring to a boil.

In a 3 qt casserole, combine beans and bacon. Stir in tomato mixture.

Bake uncovered for 1 hour at 350 degrees.

Serves 10.

We named them "Oktoberfest Beans" - but we love them anytime served with anything!

28

Beets with Pineapple

2 tbsp. brown sugar
1 tbsp. cornstarch
1/4 tsp. salt
1 small can pineapple tidbits
1 tbsp. butter or margarine
1 tbsp. lemon juice
1 14 oz. can sliced beets, drained
   or 2 cups fresh beets cooked and
   sliced

Combine brown sugar, cornstarch and
salt in a saucepan. Stir in
pineapple with juice.

Cook, stirring constantly until
mixture thickens and bubbles. Add
butter or margarine, lemon juice,
and beets.

Cook over medium heat for 5 minutes.

Serves 4 - 5

We love our beets plain, fresh from
the garden, but this one is so easy
and a gourmet veggie for beet lovers!

Broccoli Casserole

2	pkgs. frozen chopped broccoli, or 2 bunches of fresh
1	can cream of mushroom soup
2	eggs, well beaten
1	medium onion, chopped
1	cup sharp cheddar cheese, grated
1 1/2	cups stuffing mix
1/4	cup butter, melted

Cook broccoli slightly, drain and place in a greased casserole.

Combine soup, eggs and onion. Pour this mixture over the broccoli.

Sprinkle grated cheese on top.

Add melted butter to stuffing mix and put this on top.

Bake at 350 degrees for 30 minutes.

Serves 6 - 8

Broccoli – Onion Delight

1   lb. broccoli, or two 10 oz. pkgs.
    frozen broccoli spears
3   medium onions, quartered
1/4 cup butter or margarine
2   tbsp. flour
    salt and pepper to taste
1   cup milk
1   small pkg. cream cheese
1/2 cup shredded old cheddar cheese
1   cup breadcrumbs

Cut broccoli into spears and cook in
small amount of water until tender-
crisp, or cook frozen broccoli as
instructed on package, and drain.

Cook onions in small amount of water
until tender, and drain.

In saucepan, melt half of the butter
or margarine. Blend in the flour,
salt and pepper.

Add milk and cook, stirring constantly
until thickened. Blend in the cream
cheese until smooth.

Place veggies in a 2 qt. casserole,
pour sauce over and mix lightly. Top
with cheddar cheese.

Melt remaining half of the butter,
and mix with the breadcrumbs. Sprinkle
on top of casserole and bake at 350
degrees for 40 minutes or until
heated through.

Serves 6.

Louise's Broccoli Casserole

2   pkgs. chopped frozen broccoli,
     or 1 bunch of fresh broccoli
1/4 lb. velveeta cheese, grated
1/4 lb. cheddar cheese, grated
1   medium onion, chopped
1   cup sour cream

Cook broccoli until tender-crisp
and drain well.

Mix all ingredients together and
top with:

12 Ritz crackers crushed, and
1/4 cup melted butter or margarine.

Bake at 325 degrees for 30 minutes.

Serves 6.

To make velveeta or other soft
cheese easier to grate — put in
the freezer for 15 minutes!

Margie's Broccoli Casserole

2 bunches fresh broccoli, or two
   10 oz pkgs frozen broccoli spears.
1 can cream of mushroom soup
1 small container (250 ml) sour cream
1 tbsp minced onion
1 c. shredded sharp cheddar cheese
15 Ritz crackers, crushed.

Cook broccoli just until tender, or
cook frozen broccoli according to
package directions. Drain well.

Mix with all other ingredients and
bake for 20 minutes at 350 degrees.

Do not overbake.

Serves 6.

We doubled this recipe for a Dinner
Party. Everyone loved Margie's
broccoli!

Swiss Brussel Sprouts

3	10 oz. pkgs. frozen brussel sprouts, or 2 lbs. fresh
1	cup chopped onion
1/4	cup butter
2	cups finely chopped celery
3 1/2	tbsp. flour
1 2/3	cups hot milk
1/2	tsp. nutmeg
1/2	tsp. paprika
	salt and pepper to taste
1 1/2	cups grated swiss cheese
2/3	cup seasoned breadcrumbs
3	tbsp. slivered almonds
2	tbsp. butter

Cook brussel sprouts in boiling salted water until barely tender. Drain and cut in half.

Sauté onion in 1/4 cup butter until golden. Stir in celery and cook 5 min. more. Stir in flour and cook 3 min.

Remove from heat and gradually pour in milk, stirring constantly.

Return to heat and cook until thick. Add nutmeg, paprika, salt and pepper. Fold in brussel sprouts and swiss cheese.

Spoon into greased 2 qt. casserole and sprinkle with seasoned crumbs, almonds and dot with butter.

Bake at 375 degrees for 20 - 30 min. until browned and bubbly. Serves 8-10

Cabbage Casserole

3 1/2 c. sliced cabbage
1   c. chopped celery
4   tbsp butter or margarine

Sauté cabbage and celery in the butter or margarine for 10 minutes.

Place in casserole and cover with cream sauce.

Cream Sauce:

3 tbsp butter
3 tbsp flour
1 c. milk

Melt butter, add flour, add milk and cook until thickened.

Top with crushed potato chips and dot with butter.

Bake in a 350 degree over for 45 min.

This was given to us by our friend Margie who hates cabbage, but loved this!

Pennsylvania Dutch Red Cabbage

4   slices of bacon
1   medium onion, chopped
1   medium red cabbage, shredded
1   red apple, unpeeled, cored and
     cubed
1/4 c. brown sugar
1/4 c. vinegar
1   tbsp. ground cloves
     salt and pepper to taste
1/2 tsp. caraway seed
1/4 c. red wine

In large saucepan, sauté bacon
until crisp.

Remove bacon and crumble, saving
2 tbsp. drippings.

To the 2 tbsp. drippings, add all
the remaining incredients, plus the
crumbled bacon.

Cook, covered over low heat, stirring
occasionally, for 30 minutes.

Serves 12.

A local traditional dish — not just
Oktoberfest fare!
If you like cabbage, you'll _love_
this one!

Baked Carrot Casserole

6   medium carrots, grated
3   tbsps. butter
     salt and pepper to taste
3/4 tsp. sugar

In a greased casserole, layer grated carrots, salt and pepper, 1 tbsp. butter, and 1/4 tsp. sugar.

Layer 3 times until all ingredients are used.

Bake at 350 degrees for 45 minutes.

Serves 6.

If you love plain buttered carrots, you will love this make-ahead casserole.
For every extra person - just grate one more carrot!

Brandied Carrots

24 fresh baby carrots
1 oz orange-flavored liqueur or
  orange juice
3 oz lemon juice
2 oz brandy or rum
2 oz honey
1 tbsp chopped parsley

Place carrots in saucepan of cold water and bring to a boil. Simmer until tender. Drain.

Place in buttered baking dish.

Blend together liqueur, lemon juice, brandy or rum and honey and pour over carrots.

Bake for 15 minutes at 350 degrees, basting often.

Sprinkle with parsley and serve.

Serves 6.

Mother always said "carrots are good for your eyes". We say these carrots are good for your tummy!

Orange Ginger Carrots

8 medium carrots or 16 to 20
  baby carrots
1 tbsp brown sugar
1 tsp cornstarch
1/4 tsp ground ginger
1/4 tsp salt
1/4 c. orange juice
2 tbsp butter

Slice carrots crosswise 1/2 inch thick or, if using baby carrots, leave whole.

Cook in small amount of water just until tender-crisp (10 min). Drain.

In small saucepan, combine sugar, cornstarch, ginger and salt. Add orange juice. Cook stirring constantly until thick. Boil for 1 minute.

Remove from heat and stir in butter.

Pour over hot carrots and toss to coat evenly.

Garnish with parsley, if desired.

Serves 6.

Souper Glazed Carrots

In a saucepan, cook in 2 tbsp.
butter for 5 minutes:-

2 tbsp. chopped onion
1 tbsp. chopped parsley

Add:

8 large carrots, cut in 1" pieces
1 can consommé
   dash nutmeg

Cover and cook for 10 minutes.

Uncover and cook for 20 minutes
until carrots are tender and sauce
thickens and forms a glaze.

Serves 5 - 6

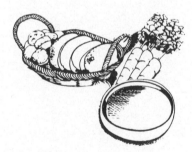

A carrot, a turnip, a pea,
Is healthy as can be!

Scalloped Cauliflower

2   10 oz packages frozen cauliflower
    or 1 large cauliflower
1   can cream of celery soup
1/2 c. milk
2   eggs, slightly beaten
1   c. shredded cheddar cheese
3/4 c. breadcrumbs
1/4 c. parsley
1/4 c. chopped pimiento
1   tbsp minced onion

Cook frozen cauliflower as directed,
or cook fresh cauliflower in small
amount of water until tender-crisp.
Drain well.

Combine soup, milk and eggs. Stir
in half of the cheddar cheese,
breadcrumbs, parsley, pimiento,
onion, and salt and pepper to taste.

Add drained cauliflower and stir
into soup mixture.

Turn into baking dish or casserole
and bake for 35 min. at 350 degrees.

Top with remaining cheddar cheese and
bake for 5 min. longer.

Serves 6 - 8

Souper Easy Cauliflower

1   medium cauliflower, or two 10 oz.
    pkgs. of frozen cauliflower
1   can cream of mushroom soup
1   cup shredded cheddar cheese
1   can drained mushrooms (optional)

Cook cauliflower until tender-crisp.

Mix soup and cheese in a greased
casserole and stir in cooked
cauliflower.

Bake for 20 minutes at 350 degrees.

Cauliflower stays white during
cooking when a piece of lemon peel
or a little milk is added to the
water.

When there's no time to make cheese
sauce for your cauliflower, this
is a life saver!

Baked Celery Casserole

4   cups celery cut diagonally into
        bite-size pieces
1   can water chestnuts, drained and
        cut in half
1/2 cup diced pimiento (optional)
1   can cream of chicken soup
1   tbsp. butter
1/2 cup breadcrumbs
        slivered almonds

Mix all ingredients together and
place in a greased casserole dish.

Sauté breadcrumbs in 1 tablespoon
of butter and spoon on top.

Sprinkle with slivered almonds.

Bake, covered, at 350 degrees for
25 minutes, and then uncovered for
15 minutes.

Serves 6

Cheesey Garden Casserole

1   pkg. (7 1/4 oz.) long grain and
     wild rice
3   cups zucchini, sliced
1   green pepper, sliced
1   medium onion, sliced
1   can sliced mushrooms, drained
2   cups spaghetti sauce
2   cups shredded cheddar cheese
1   cup shredded swiss cheese

Cook rice according to package
directions.

Simmer sliced vegetables together
until just tender. Drain well.

Place 1/2 of rice in a greased
8 X 12 casserole dish.

Spoon 1/2 of vegetables over rice.

Sprinkle with shredded cheddar cheese
and 1/2 of the spaghetti sauce.

Layer rice, vegetables and rest of
spaghetti sauce again.

Top with shredded swiss cheese.

Bake, uncovered, for 35 minutes at
375 degrees.

Serves 10.

Our favorite veggie casserole!
A real winner! Brings raves whether
served with a steak or a hamburger.

Baked Corn and Swiss Cheese

1   19 oz. can whole kernel corn, drained
1   small can evaporated milk
1   cup shredded swiss cheese
2   beaten eggs
2   - 3 green onions, chopped
    dash pepper
1   cup soft bread crumbs
2   tbsp. butter melted.

Combine corn, evaporated milk, 3/4 cup shredded cheese, eggs, chopped onion and dash of pepper.

Turn mixture into greased 1 qt. casserole.

Toss bread crumbs with melted butter and 1/4 cup shredded cheese.

Sprinkle over corn mixture.

Bake for 30 min. at 350 degrees.

Serves 4 - 6

A welcome change from plain canned corn. Almost a soufflé!

Baked Corn & Tomatoes

1   12 oz. can corn niblets
1   19 oz. can stewed tomatoes
1/2 green pepper, chopped
1/2 tsp. salt
1/4 tsp. pepper
1/2 tsp. sugar
3/4 cup fresh breadcrumbs
1   tbsp. butter or margarine

Drain corn and tomatoes.

Mix chopped green pepper and
seasonings with corn and tomatoes
and pour into a greased 1 1/2 qt.
casserole.

Sprinkle crumbs on top and dot with
butter or margarine.

Bake for 30 minutes at 350 degrees.

Serves 4.

Fast and easy - a great combination!

Eggplant Parmesan

1   medium eggplant, unpeeled and sliced 1/2" thick
1   egg, beaten
1/2 cup fine, dry breadcrumbs
1/4 cup oil
    salt and pepper to taste
1   14 oz. can spaghetti sauce
2   cups grated mozzarella cheese
    parmesan cheese

Use two pie plates – one for the beaten egg, and one for the crumbs.

Dip eggplant slices into beaten egg and then into crumbs.

Heat oil and brown eggplant well on both sides.

Place slices in single layer in large baking pan and season with salt and pepper.

Pour spaghetti sauce over eggplant and top with the mozzarella cheese.

Sprinkle with parmesan cheese.

Bake for 30 minutes at 350 degrees.

A nice, easy, versatile eggplant casserole.
Serve at your next barbecue!

Mushroom Mania

```
1 1/2  lbs. fresh sliced mushrooms
6      slices buttered white bread
1/2    cup chopped onion
1/2    cup chopped celery
1/2    cup chopped green pepper
1/2    cup mayonnaise
3/4    tsp. salt
1/4    tsp. pepper
2      eggs, slightly beaten
1 1/2  cups milk
1      can cream of mushroom soup
       grated cheddar cheese
       croutons
```

Sauté mushrooms in butter until barely cooked.

Cube 3 slices of bread and arrange them in a casserole.

Combine mushrooms with the onion, celery, green pepper, mayonnaise, salt and pepper, and put the mixture on top of the bread.

Cube remaining 3 slices of bread and layer them on the mushroom mixture.

Beat eggs with 1 1/2 cups of milk and pour over everything. Refrigerate at least one hour.

One hour before serving, pour a can of undiluted mushroom soup over it and top with a sprinkling of croutons.

Bake at 300 degrees for 60 min. Ten minutes before end of baking time, sprinkle grated cheese on top. Serves 6.

Honey Glazed Parsnips and Carrots

3 medium carrots, sliced 1" thick
3 medium parsnips, sliced 1" thick
2 tbsp. honey
1 tbsp. butter
   Rind of 1/2 orange and the juice,
   or 2 tbsp. orange juice.

In saucepan, cook parsnips and
carrots in small amount of boiling,
salted water until tender-crisp. Drain.

Add honey, butter, orange rind and
orange juice.

Cook over medium heat, stirring
occasionally, until veggies are
glazed.

Serves 4.

This team's a winner!

Honey - Orange Parsnips

4   medium parsnips, peeled and sliced
3   tbsp. butter or margarine
1   tbsp. honey
1   tsp. grated orange rind
3   tbsp. orange juice

Cook parsnips in boiling water until tender-crisp. Drain.

Combine remaining ingredients and pour over parsnips.

Simmer, stirring occasionally, until sauce is reduced and parsnips are glazed.

Serves 4.

If your family rejects parsnips - like ours, try these, they're marvellous!

Canton Peas

2	10 oz. pkgs. frozen peas
1	can mushrooms, drained
1	can water chestnuts, drained and sliced
1	c. chopped green onion
3/4	tsp. ginger
1/4	tsp. nutmeg
1	c. chicken broth or consommé
2	tbsp. cornstarch
1	tsp. salt
1/8	tsp. pepper
1/8	tsp. garlic powder

In saucepan, separate peas.

Add mushrooms, water chestnuts, onion, ginger, nutmeg and 3/4 cup broth. Cover and simmer for 3 - 4 minutes.

In a cup, mix cornstarch and remaining 1/4 cup of broth until smooth. Stir into peas.

Cook, stirring constantly, until liquid boils and thickens.

Add salt, garlic powder and pepper.

Serves 6 - 8

Creamed Peas

2   tbsp. butter
2   tbsp. chopped green onion
1   tbsp. flour
1   tsp. sugar
    pinch thyme
    pinch nutmeg
1/2 tsp. salt
    dash pepper
3/4 cup milk
2   10 oz. packages frozen peas

Melt butter. Add onion and cook gently, stirring constantly for 5 min.

Add flour, sugar, thyme, nutmeg, salt and pepper. Stir to blend and remove from heat.

Add milk, stir and return to moderate heat. Cook, stirring constantly, until boiling, thickened and smooth. Turn heat to low and cook, stirring occasionally, for 10 minutes.

Cook peas in boiling salted water until tender-crisp. Drain.

Stir in hot sauce.

Serves 6 - 8

No veggie book is complete without creamed peas. Good on toast or served in tiny tart shells!

Quick Oven Peas

1   20 oz. package of frozen peas
1   can sliced mushrooms, drained
1/4 cup chopped onion
2   tbsps. butter
1/4 tsp. dried savoury
1   tbsp. water
     salt and pepper to taste

Place all ingredients in a 1 1/2 qt. casserole.

Cover and bake at 350 degrees for 40 - 45 minutes, until peas are tender, stirring after 20 minutes.

Serves 8.

Quick Creamy Peas

Cook and drain a 10 oz. package of frozen peas.

Stir in 1/2 cup sour cream, pinch of celery salt, pinch of dry mustard, and pepper to taste.

Serves 4.

Hash Brown Potato Casserole

2   lbs. frozen hash brown potatoes
1   cup diced onion
1   can cream of mushroom soup, or
       cream of chicken soup.
1   large carton (500 ml) sour
       cream
1/4   cup margarine, melted
2   cups grated cheddar cheese
       crushed potato chips

Place soup, sour cream, margarine
and cheese in saucepan and simmer
until well blended.

Mix with frozen hash brown potatoes
and onion.

Place in very large greased casserole
or two smaller ones.

Sprinkle crushed potato chips on top
and bake in 375 degree oven for one
hour.

Serves 12

We've made these hash browns for years!
Try them with your Easter ham or your
next Champagne breakfast.
Try them in a foil pan on your
barbecue!

Make Ahead Mashed Potatoes

9   large potatoes
1   large pkg. (250 g.) cream cheese
    softened
1   c. sour cream
2   tsp. onion salt
1   tsp. salt
    dash pepper
2   tbsp. butter
1   egg, beaten

Cook potatoes in boiling water until
tender. Drain.

Mash well and add the rest of the
ingredients. Beat until fluffy.

Let cool slightly and place in large,
greased casserole. Dot with more
butter and refrigerate.

To serve, remove from the refrigerator
1 hour before serving and bake
uncovered at 350 degrees for 30 min.
or until heated through.

Serves 12.

This may be prepared 5 days ahead and
refrigerated until ready to use.
May also be frozen, but thaw completely
before heating.

No last minute mashing!
Even mashed potatoes may be made ahead!

Mary Ellen's Cheese & Potato Bake

```
6     medium potatoes, boiled
      salt and pepper to taste
2     large tomatoes
1     tsp. dried basil
1/2   lb. mozzarella cheese
1/3   cup chopped parsley
1/3   cup parmesan cheese
1/4   cup melted butter
```

Cut potatoes in 1/2" slices and arrange in single layer in buttered 9 X 13 baking pan.

Season with salt and pepper.

Slice tomatoes and arrange on top of potatoes.

Sprinkle with basil and more salt and pepper to taste.

Top with shredded mozzarella cheese, parsley and parmesan cheese.

Drizzle melted butter over all.

Bake at 350 degrees for 25 minutes.

Serves 6.

Oven French Fries For Two

Heat oven to 450 – 475 degrees.

Scrub 1 large potato (unpeeled) and cut in half lengthwise.

Cut each half into 8 fingers and toss fingers in 1 tbsp. oil.

Place on cookie sheet, not touching.

Bake for 20 to 25 minutes, turning once.

Sprinkle with salt, pepper and paprika.

Too good for two!
Make more – you'll never buy frozen again!

Sweet Potato Casserole

4   cups, hot, mashed sweet
        potatoes
1/4   cup butter or margarine
1/2   tsp. salt
1/4   cup orange juice
2   cups miniature marshmallows

Combine sweet potatoes with butter
or margarine, salt, orange juice
and 1 cup of marshmallows.

Place in a greased 1 1/2 qt.
casserole.

Dot with remaining cup of marshmallows
and bake at 350 degrees for 30 min.

Sweet Potatoes In Orange Sauce

8 medium sweet potatoes

Cook sweet potatoes and cool.

Slice and arrange in a greased casserole.

Sauce::

2 tbsp. cornstarch
1 cup brown sugar
1/2 tsp. salt
2 tbsp. grated orange peel
1/4 cup butter or margarine
2 cups fresh orange juice

Combine all ingredients and cook until thick.

Pour over sweet potatoes.

Bake at 350 degrees for 30 minutes.

Serves 10 - 12

Fanny's Sweet Potato Casserole

3   cups sweet potatoes, mashed, or
      3 large sweet potatoes, cooked
      and mashed
1/3 cup half and half cream, or milk
1/2 cup butter
2/3 cup white sugar
2   eggs, slightly beaten
1   tsp. vanilla

Mix all ingredients together and pour into a buttered casserole.

Topping:

1   cup brown sugar
1/2 cup flour
1/3 cup melted butter
1   cup chopped pecans

Mix topping ingredients together with a fork.

Sprinkle topping mixture on sweet potatoes.

Bake at 350 degrees for 30 - 35 min.

Serves 6

Use less sugar if you like ----
but don't tell Fanny!

Yams and Pommes

2   cans sweet potatoes or 6 medium
      sweet potatoes
2   medium tart apples
1/2 cup brown sugar
      salt and pepper to taste
3/4 tsp. nutmeg
1/2 tsp. cinnamon
1/4 cup melted butter
1/2 cup orange juice
2   tbsp. lemon juice
1   tbsp. prepared mustard
1/3 cup seedless raisins
1/3 cup chopped pecans

Slice sweet potatoes, or cook fresh
sweet potatoes until tender, drain
and slice.

Pare, core and slice apples.

In a greased casserole, layer
potatoes and apples, ending with
apples.

Sprinkle each layer with sugar, salt
and pepper, nutmeg and cinnamon.

Mix melted butter, orange juice and
lemon juice, and mustard. Pour over
top.

Sprinkle with raisins and pecans.

Bake at 350 degrees for 40 minutes.

Serves 8

Bouillon Rice

1 1/2 c. rice
1   can mushrooms, drained, or
        sauté 1/2 lb. fresh mushrooms
        in 1/4 c. butter
1   can beef broth
1   can onion soup
1/4   c. butter or margarine

Mix all ingredients together and
place in casserole.

Bake uncovered for 60 minutes at
350 degrees, stirring after 30 min.

Serves 6.

You may use 2 cans of chicken broth
instead of 1 can of beef broth and
1 can of onion soup and serve with
chicken or pork.

Delicious with Prime Rib or Steak.

Carol's Spinach Ricotta Pie

1	9" unbaked pie shell
2	green onions, chopped
2	tbsp. butter
1	bag of spinach, washed, drained and broken, or 1 pkg. frozen spinach, cooked and drained well
3	eggs
1/2	cup light cream
1	cup ricotta cheese
1/2	cup shredded Farmers or mild cheese
	salt and pepper to taste

Sauté onions in butter. Add spinach and sauté.

Beat eggs, cream, ricotta and mild cheese.

Add spinach, onions, salt and pepper to taste, and beat with electric mixer.

Pour into pie shell and bake at 375 degrees for 30 minutes.

You may top with more mild cheese, if desired.

Serves 6

Laurel's Spinach Casserole

1   10 oz. pkg. frozen spinach, or
    1 bag of fresh spinach
1/2 cup sour cream
1/4 pkg. dry onion soup mix
1   egg, slightly beaten

Partially cook spinach and drain well.

Mix sour cream, dry onion soup mix and slightly beaten egg together and fold in spinach.

Bake in a greased casserole for 30 minutes at 350 degrees.

Serves 4

Laurel says this is how to get your kids to eat their spinach!

Spinach and Mushrooms

2   bags of fresh spinach
3/4 - 1 pound fresh mushrooms
3   tbsp. bacon fat or cooking oil
1 1/2 c. grated old cheddar cheese
1/4   c. sherry

Wash and trim spinach. Place in a
large saucepan and bring to a boil.
Cook 5 minutes and drain well.

Wash and slice mushrooms and sauté
in bacon fat or oil for 10 minutes.

Layer spinach, mushrooms, cheese and
sherry in a 2 qt. greased casserole
until all ingredients are used,
ending with a layer of cheese and
sherry.

Bake uncovered for 30 minutes at
350 degrees.

Serves 6.

Popeye loves spinach - now you
will too!

Yellow Squash Casserole

2   lbs. yellow squash, sliced
1   onion, chopped
2   large carrots, grated
1   can cream of chicken soup
1   c. dairy sour cream
1   tsp. salt
1/4 tsp. pepper
1/4 c. butter or margarine, melted
8   oz. seasoned bread crumbs
     paprika (optional)

In saucepan cook squash and onion in boiling salted water until tender. Drain. May be mashed or left in slices.

Combine cream of chicken soup, sour cream, salt and pepper. Mix well.

Stir in grated carrot. Fold in squash and onion.

Combine butter and seasoned crumbs.

Sprinkle half of the crumb mixture in a buttered 2 1/2 qt. casserole. Pour squash mixture over and top with remaining crumb mixture. Sprinkle with paprika and bake at 350 degrees for 30 - 45 min. until heated through - or -

Pour squash mixture into casserole and top with buttered crumbs and bake as directed.

Really good! The best squash casserole we tried.

Marilyn's Scalloped Tomatoes & Herbs

2	medium onions, sliced
1 1/2	tsp. sugar
1/2	tsp. salt
1/4	tsp. pepper
1/2	tsp. thyme
1/4	cup butter, melted
1	28 oz. can tomatoes
2	tbsp. butter
2	cups coarse, soft breadcrumbs
1	tsp. chopped chives
2	tbsp. chopped parsley

Sauté onions, sugar, salt, pepper and thyme in 1/4 cup butter until onions are transparent.

Drain tomatoes and chop.

Mix breadcrumbs, chives and parsley, and add 1/2 of this mixture to the onions.

Layer tomatoes and onion and crumb mixture, ending with tomatoes.

Top with the other half of the crumbs and dot with the 2 tbsp. butter.

Bake uncovered at 350 degrees for 45 minutes.

Top should be crispy.

Stuck for a veggie? Goes well with everything!

67

Festive Turnip

1   large turnip
2   good cooking apples
    (courtland, spy)
2   tbsp. butter
1/4 c. brown sugar
    dash cinnamon

Topping:

1/3 c. brown sugar
1/3 c. flour
2   tbsp. butter

Peel and dice turnip. Cook in boiling water until tender. Drain and mash with butter.

Peel and slice apples and mix with the brown sugar and cinnamon.

In a greased casserole, layer 1/2 the turnip, then the apple and then the remaining turnip.

Put brown sugar and flour in a small bowl and cut in the butter until crumbly. Sprinkle on top of turnip and bake at 350 degrees for 1 hour.

Serves 8

This is our traditional "Christmas" dinner turnip.

Turnips & Veggies Au Gratin

1 1/4	cups boiling water
1	tsp. salt
1	small turnip cut into finger strips
1	large onion, quartered
1	cup celery cut into 1/2 inch slices
1/2	green pepper, cut into strips
2	tbsp. cornstarch
1/4	cup cold water
1	tbsp. butter
1/2	cup grated cheddar cheese

Bring water to boil and add salt. Add turnip and onion and cook gently, covered, for 15 min. Then add celery and green pepper and cook until all are tender-crisp.

Drain and reserve liquid in another pot. Keep drained vegetables warm. (You should have 1 cup of drained liquid).

Stir cornstarch with 1/4 cup cold water and make a paste. Add to reserved liquid.

Stir in cheese and butter. Stir until melted and add veggies.

Heat thoroughly.

Serves 6.

A little more effort, but well worth it!

Veggie Casserole

1   large onion, sliced
2   10 oz. pkgs. frozen chopped
    broccoli, cooked and well
    drained.
2   cans small carrots, drained, or
    1/2 lb. frozen baby carrots cooked
    and well drained
1   can sliced mushrooms, drained, or
    1 lb. fresh mushrooms sliced and
    cooked in 2 tbsp. butter
1   can cream of mushroom soup
1   can cream of celery soup

Mix vegetables together and pour
soups over, mixing well.

Top with 1 cup of shredded cheddar
cheese.

Bake at 350 degrees for 30 - 45 min.

Serves 6 - 8

A nice veggie medley.   Freezes well!

Veggie Moussaka

1 medium eggplant
1 tsp. salt
1/2 c. vegetable oil
3 medium zucchini
2 medium onions
1 28 oz. can whole tomatoes
  salt and pepper to taste
2 cloves garlic, minced
1/2 lb. penne noodles
1/4 c. milk
1 egg, slightly beaten
1/2 c. parmesan cheese
2 tbsp. parsley
2 c. shredded mozzarella or
  swiss cheese.

Peel eggplant and slice in 1/4 inch slices. Place on oiled cookie sheet and drizzle with 1/4 cup oil. Broil until golden. Turn and brown the other side. Remove and set aside.

Slize zucchini lengthwise into 1/4 inch slices. Place on cookie sheet and drizzle with remaining 1/4 cup oil. Brown until golden. Turn and brown the other side. Remove and set aside.

Brown onions and garlic in small amount of oil until transparent. Remove and set aside.

Drain tomatoes, reserving juice. Slice tomatoes. Add salt and pepper to juice.

(continued on next page)

Veggie Moussaka - continued

Cook noodles according to package directions and drain.

Mix 1/4 cup milk with beaten egg and pour over cooked noodles. Mix well.

In a greased 9 X 13 baking dish, layer noodle mixture, parmesan cheese, eggplant, onions and garlic, parsley, zucchini, sliced tomatoes, tomato juice and mozzarella or swiss cheese.

Bake at 350 degrees for 30 minutes.

Serves 12.

A little more preparation but well worth the effort!

Veggie Spaghetti Sauce

1/4 c. olive oil
2   tbsp. butter
2   large ripe tomatoes, chopped
1   small onion, chopped
1   cup zucchini, diced (1 small)
1   cup eggplant, diced
1   medium red pepper, sliced, or
    1 medium green pepper, sliced,
    or both
2   cloves garlic, finely chopped
1   cup meatless spaghetti sauce

Sauté tomatoes, onion, zucchini,
eggplant, pepper and garlic in oil
and butter on medium heat for 10 min.
or until veggies are tender.

Add spaghetti sauce to veggies and
simmer for 10 minutes.

Season with salt and pepper to taste.

Serve over warm spaghetti and sprinkle
with grated parmesan cheese.

1 lb. spaghetti and sauce should
serve 4 - 6.

We all loved this meatless Spaghetti
Sauce! A vegetarian's delight!

Stuffed Zucchini

4	zucchini, 6" - 7" long
1 3/4	cups soft breadcrumbs
1/2	cup grated cheddar cheese
1/4	cup chopped onion
2	tbsp. chopped parsley
	salt and pepper to taste
2	eggs, beaten
1/4	tsp. salt
2	tbsp. butter
1/2	cup grated parmesan cheese

Scrub zucchini well. Cut off ends but do not peel.

Cook in 2 cups of boiling, salted water. Do not overcook. Drain.

Cut zucchini in half lengthwise and carefully remove center part with tip of a spoon.

Turn zucchini hollow side down on paper towels to drain.

Chop center part of zucchini and combine with crumbs, grated cheese, chopped onion, parsley, salt and pepper, and eggs.

Place zucchini hollow side up in a greased 9 X 13 baking pan. Sprinkle with 1/4 tsp. salt.

Fill with bread mixture. Dot with butter and sprinkle with parmesan cheese. Bake at 350 degrees for 35 - 45 min, or until browned on top.

Serves 8

Tomato Zucchini Casserole

1   cup grated cheddar cheese
1/3   cup grated parmesan cheese
1   tsp. chopped fresh oregano
1   tsp. chopped fresh basil
                or
       1/2 tsp. each, crushed, dried
1   clove garlic, minced
1/2   tsp. salt
1/4   tsp. freshly ground pepper
3   medium zucchini, sliced
2   large tomatoes, sliced
1/4   cup butter
2   tbsp. finely chopped onions
1/2   cup breadcrumbs

Combine cheddar, parmesan, herbs, garlic, salt and pepper.

Butter an 8" square or 2 litre casserole.

Arrange half of the zucchini slices in casserole. Sprinkle with 1/4 of the cheese mixture.

Arrange half of sliced tomatoes on top and sprinkle with 1/4 of cheese mixture. Repeat this again.

In a small skillet, melt butter and sauté onions until transparent. Add breadcrumbs and stir until they absorb butter. Spread on top of casserole.

Cover and bake at 375 degrees for 30 min. Uncover and bake 20 - 25 min. or until top is crusty and vegetables are tender. Serves 6.

Metric Conversion

Spoons   Rounded

1/4 teaspoon	1 ml
1/2 teaspoon	2 ml
1 teaspoon	5 ml
2 teaspoons	10 ml
1 tablespoon	15 ml

Cups

1/4 cup	50 ml
1/3 cup	75 ml
1/2 cup	125 ml
2/3 cup	150 ml
3/4 cup	175 ml
1 cup	250 ml

Ounces

1 oz.	30 grams
2 oz.	55 grams
3 oz.	85 grams
4 oz.	115 grams
5 oz.	140 grams
6 oz.	170 grams
7 oz.	200 grams
8 oz.	250 grams
16 oz.	500 grams
32 oz.	1 kg

A Great Idea For:

Showers, bridge prizes, stocking stuffers, host or hostess gift, or just an inexpensive gift for veggie lovers!

Please send me:

_____ copies of Muffin Mania at $6.95 per copy

_____ copies of La Manie des Muffins at $6.95 per copy

_____ copies of Nibble Mania at $6.95 per copy

_____ copies of Veggie Mania at $6.95 per copy

Plus $1.00 per copy for mailing.

Enclosed is $_____

Name_____

Street_____

City_____

Province_____ Postal Code_____

Make cheque payable to:

Muffin Mania Publishing Co., c/o Mrs. Cathy Prange, 184 Lydia St., Kitchener, Ont. N2H 1W1

Notes

notes

notes